A B C D E F G H I J K L M N O P Q R S T U V W X Y Z

Underwater A to Z

Elspeth Graham

Oxford

a b c d e f g h i j k l m n o p q r s t u v w x y z

angel fish

coral

butterfly fish

dolphin

eels

fire fish

goldfish

hermit crab

Indian
glassfish

jelly fish

kissing
gourami fish

lobster

mandarin
fish

needlefish

octopus

pipe fish

queen fish

ray

seahorse

N O P **Q** **R** **S** **T** **U** V W X Y Z

turtle ▶

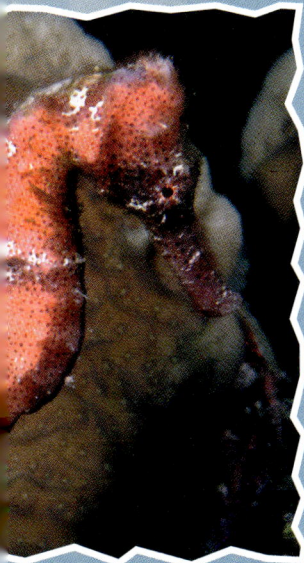

upside-down
catfish ▶

viper fish

winkle

x-ray fish

yellowhead
jawfish

zebra eel

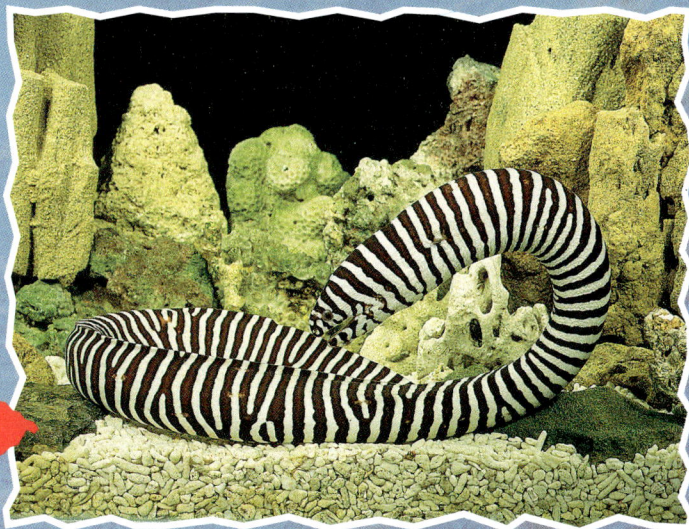

Oxford University Press, Great Clarendon Street, Oxford, OX2 6DP

Oxford New York
Athens Auckland Bangkok Bogota Buenos Aires
Calcutta Cape Town Chennai Dar es Salaam Delhi
Florence Hong Kong Istanbul Karachi Kuala Lumpur
Madrid Melbourne Mexico City Mumbai Nairobi Paris
São Paulo Singapore Taipei Tokyo Toronto Warsaw

and associated companies in
Berlin Ibadan

Oxford is a trade mark of Oxford University Press

ISBN 0 19 915766 9
Available in packs
Pack B Pack of Six   (one of each book)   ISBN 0 19 915771 5
Pack B Class Pack   (six of each book)   ISBN 0 19 915772 3

Acknowledgements

The publisher would like to thank the following for permission
to reproduce photographs: Bruce Coleman/Jane Burton p 6,
Bruce Coleman p 7 (centre); Heather Angel pp 3, 9, 10; NHPA
p 10: Oxford Scientific Films/Richard Kolar p 4 (bottom), Oxford
Scientific Films/Max Gibbs pp 4 (top), 5 (top), 7 (top), 10 (centre),
11 (bottom).

All other photography by Corel Professional Photos.

Printed in Hong Kong